NOT TABOO

Lisa Monaghan

BookLeaf Publishing

Presentation by *BookLeaf Publishing*

Web: www.bookleafpub.com

E-mail: info@bookleafpub.com

ISBN : 9789357699259

First edition 2022

Presentation by *BookLeaf Publishing*

Web: www.bookleafpub.com

E-mail: info@bookleafpub.com

ISBN : 9789357699259

First edition 2022

PREFACE

Hey guys,

I wanted to create a book of poetry on the subjects that are still kind of taboo and not spoken about openly enough. I hope by publishing this book of poetry it will encourage people to open up, talk, help educate and even bring comfort to people.

I am a person who tries to help people where I can and if this book of poetry can help one person feel better or feel like they are not alone then it is worth it. I hope it is a reminder to be #kind and hopefully bring everyone together once again.

I feel there is so much pain and suffering in the world and we do not need any more of that so let's talk about the things not spoken about enough, lets encourage normalising talking and open up on the difficult stuff and let us support and love one another. Is that not what life is about?

X

Taboo

Let's talk about topics that are still kind of
taboo…
As we need to talk about them, we really do…
Mental health…
And taking care of one's self…
Let's normalise talking and sharing…
Coming together and caring…
Talking about those subjects and daring…
To stand up and speak our truth and how we
really feel inside…
Mental health is no easy ride…
Even if it's just no I'm not ok, I tried…

Abuse

Emotional abuse comes in lots of ways…
Victims live with this day to day…
Whether it be from parents, siblings, partners or friends…
Look through the eyes of the victim lens…
The way it destroys you…
Crying on the loo…
Mentally broken and do not know what to do…
And feel you have nobody to reach out too…
No matter who the abuser it is never ok…
Made to suffer and live with this day to day…
Please tell someone and speak up ok…
You did not deserve this…
Please believe me sir or miss…
This was not your fault…
No abuse is ok, even mental assault…
It takes away everything from you…
Especially narcissist abuse that is true…
Left desperate and alone and don't know what to do…
It sucks your confidence and destroys your self esteem…
Mentally broken and want to scream…
That gorgeous smile gone which once forever beamed…
But I promise you, you can get that back…

You will rebuild yourself and get back on
track…
You will heal from the trauma and pain…
And all that drove you insane…
It will take time to fix the broken pieces back
together…
But once you have done it your be stronger than
ever…
The first step is to reach out…
Do not listen to the self doubt…
Or making excuses and feeling like this is your
fault...
Nobody deserves physical or mental assault...
In the end you are the only one suffering and in
pain…
Manipulating control is their gain...
You can do this and deserve better you really
do…
So be brave and open up to a friend is what you
need to do…
You do not deserve this abuse it's driving you
round the bend…
Get out now and get the help you need to
mend…
Please reach out you can do this…
I promise you this…

Sexuality

Is it normal to feel this way?…
A girl who likes girls and a boy who likes boys
is that ok?…
Does that make me gay?…
These are the questions a lot of people ask
themselves day to day…
Scared to come out worried what will people
say?…
What will my parents say…
I want you to know it is ok to be scared and feel
this way…
The important thing is to talk to someone who
you trust…
If you are depressed and low, this is a must…
Not knowing who you like is normal and not
everybody knows right away…
So, it is ok to not be sure or bisexual ok…
We all seem to think we should have everything
figured out…
Like we should know ourselves and what life is
about…
Sometimes it takes years and years to get to
know who you are…
Learning, experimenting, growing and accepting
who you are will get you far…
So, it is ok to not be sure and little insecure…

There is no crime in being unsure…
If you ever feel like you are not normal or do not fit in…
Or like you are committing a sin…
Then put those thoughts right in the bin…
Because you are amazing just as you…
You know who you are deep down you really do…
You are strong…
Nothing about you is wrong…
Do not ever give up because you are amazing just as you are…
You have so much to offer the world and will go so far…
You have been strong for so long…
It is ok to be brave, be you and dance to your own lifes song…
One day you will realise you knew you could do this all along…

Religion

When did we all turn on each other for what we believed in?…
Isn't anger, violence and hurting others a sin?…
Violence, bombings, stabbings, terrorism and hurting others day to day…
Would our gods and who we pray to think this is ok?…
Why are we hurting each other?…
That is someone's father, sister or mother…
Since when was religion about suffering and pain…
Tearing each other part and driving people insane…
In the end we all believe in a higher being and praying so are we not all the same?…
Religion should bring us closer together not drive us apart or cause hate…
How we live our life and help others is that not our true fate?…
So let us say it is ok to have different religions and prayers…
So long as we respect each other, love and care…
Let's not cause any more destruction or despair…

Can we accept we all have different beliefs but still love each other, is that fair?…

Addiction

Drug addiction…
Alcohol addiction…
Sexual addiction…
Food addiction…
They are all the same…
Tearing families apart and causing lots of pain…
But the person is not to blame…
Addiction is the same as a mental illness but does not receive the same media fame…
It causes such destruction and heartache…
Do we not need to raise more awareness for others sakes?…
We judge what we see…
Not the actions crying please help me…
More awareness of self destruction and addiction is needed…
Many have pleaded…
With help beating addiction lots have succeeded…
So, if you are an addict of any kind…
Please know there is help to find…
Please open up and bare this in mind…
You are not your addiction you can beat this I believe in you…
Open up to someone is the first step you really need to do…

It won't be easy…
Nothing worth having is easy peasy…
It will be very tough…
At times your want to quit and have enough…
But keeping your family and friends is that not the motivation light?…
Keep that in your mind that beautiful sight…
You can beat the fight…
You can rebuild your life and you…
You just need to put the work in and commitment too…
Anything can be repaired…
More hurt and pain spared…
You are stronger than you know…
You can really beat this all time low…
I believe in you so much…
Please open up and take that helping hand touch…

Suicide

Why is it people think suicide is cowardly and the easy way out…
I never understood what that was all about…
To be so upset you want to end your life I think takes such strength…
To take that step and be so sad to go to these lengths…
To think how people feel they have no other way out…
Full of hopelessness and such self doubt…
Makes me feel sad to know someone felt they had no choice but to give up and go…
And struggled to cope with the day to day flow…
It is incredibly painful and sad…
Knowing once they made this decision they were glad…
Suicide is not cowardly so let us stop being mad…
Instead let us normalise talking and opening up…
Calling each other and asking what's up…
Checking on that colleague, family or friend…
A friend missing, a quick text we need to send…
Notice if someone is missing from the pub or group that day…

Calling and asking them if they are ok…
Let us make it a habit to say I am not ok and feel sad…
Let's not make each other feel bad…
Let us greet everyone with kindness…
Encouraging hugs and mindfulness…
Online let's be kind…
Trolling and negative comments can contribute and stay in someone's mind…
And make them feel mad…
Then feel sad…
So let us stop being mean…
Make others feel heard and seen…
Support one another, listen, talk to our children and teens…
Supportive community family where have we been…

Loneliness

I sit here all alone…
Nobody to call and nobody picks up the phone…
Family and friends there but sometimes only moan…
Isolation is a real issue for many people no matter your age…
Four walls closing in like a cage…
The sound of silence is so loud…
Enjoying my own company, I should be proud…
Being independent is great…
And such an amazing trait…
But some people do not have any mates…
And all alone everyday…
Living the same routine day to day…
Even children wishing they had friends to go out with and play…
Sometimes you can be in a room full of people and have constant texts and calls on your phone…
But still feel all alone…
Loneliness does not discriminate and can affect all…
Men lonely but scared to speak up in case they feel like fools…

So, I want you to know, I know what it is like to feel all alone…
It really is ok to cry and moan…
But please do call someone and pick up the phone…
It is ok to only have yourself and you…
I understand I really do…
I promise you I have been there too…
But everyone needs a friend…
To help you while you are a bit broken and help mend…
So, write that text and send…
I am lonely can you help me…
And watch everyone will want to be your friend let's see…

Miscarriage

I have lost a big part of me…
How did this happen I was a mum to be…
My beautiful baby I will never see…
Single or with a partner you feel all alone…
Not wanting to see anyone or pick up the phone…
People think early pregnancy loss is not the same…
And one of those things and nobody is to blame…
But a loss is a loss no matter how far along…
Babies with their mothers is where they belong…
Saying goodbye crushes your soul and heart…
It is ok to fall apart…
But slowly trying to rebuild yourself is a good start…
It is ok to mourn and there is no timeline for healing…
It's ok to exist and simply just being…
Just make sure you let others support you…
Do not hide away it is others pain too…
You will feel better I promise you…
Your angel baby with you forever that is true…

Racism

Racism is a crime…
Yet racist comments happen time after time…
It is still very much an issue day to day…
Racist comments online, people like and think it is ok…
Nelson Mandela did not fight for this to continue ok…
Why do we judge people by skin colour still…
Black, Asian or white what is the big deal…
It is inside what counts…
Not our skin colour or the money in our bank accounts…
So much discrimination in the world we see…
I am who I am I can only be me…
Let us take a stand, as Black Lives Matter too…
Saying no to racism is what we really need to do…
Let us teach our children to love each other as we are all the same inside that is true…

Disability

They stood and laughed at that person walking funny…
Not knowing their life is tough and not always sunny…
They stood and tutted whilst that child screamed…
Not knowing this child had autism and is not what it seemed…
They mocked that person in a wheelchair…
Whilst then thought why me? This is not fair…
They stood and laughed and did not care…
They shouted nasty comments at that person who is blind…
Not knowing life is hard and not always kind…
They mocked that person with a missing limb or two…
Not knowing that person nearly died for their country that is true…
They really had no clue…
They did not realise their laughs, jokes and comments hurt these people deep inside…
And that they went home and cried…
Wishing they did not go out that day or try…
When did we start to laugh at others misfortunes and pain?…
Did we all just go insane?…

Since when did hurting someone else become
our gain…
You really never know what people are dealing
with…
We should all be supporting each other and
wanting to give…
Nothing but positive, helpful comments and a
helping hand…
As it is easy for someone to feel like they are
drowning in quick sand…
So, if you cannot say anything nice at all…
Stay quiet, smile and don't be a fool…

Crime

Do you ever worry for your children and what they get up to…
Hoping they make good choices in everything that they do…
And hoping they do not mix with the wrong people that is true…
As parents we lay awake at night worried about gangs and knife crime…
Wondering what our children are doing half the time…
Whilst we cannot wrap them in cotton wool as much as we want too…
Educating them to be safe and behave is what we really need to do…
Showing them the dangers out there…
Hoping they will listen and showing them we only care…
Trying to promote independence but still worried and still trying to be fair…
Teenage crime is on the rise…
Children telling parents lies…
Where they really are at night…
Hoping they are not getting into fights…
Educate your children about crime, the law and dangers of society…

Hoping they will listen and make being safe a priority…

Bullying

Teach our children bullying is never ok…
Drum it in to them every day…
Encourage our children to let other children play…
Teach them to be kind…
With a gentle and caring mind…
If they see another child sad…
Talk to them they will be glad…
Let us teach our children to speak up if they are being bullied one day…
Encourage them to speak up and let them know that it is ok…
Tell them if friends ask you to be mean to another…
Go tell a teacher or your mother…
Teach our children to say bullying is a no…
It is never ok to make another person feel so low…
Stop bullying full stop it is a NO...

Online Dating In 2022

Online dating...
Is very frustrating…
Constant Psycho fears...
And all we hear...
Tall or a shorty…
Better be under forty…
Fat or skinny…
Magazines convincing us we need to be proper skinny Minnie's…
Send us a pic…
Inbox flooded with pics of dicks…
You are the only one I am chatting too…
I wouldn't lie to you that's true…
They think we are fools they really do…
All we here is I do not like texting…
Only if it involves sexting…
Crazy stalker guys…
Married, cheaters, games and lies…
We give up and only sigh…
Online dating is a mine field that is true…
Hard to meet people day to day if busy so what else can we do…
The weirdos and the fakes…
Sort yourself out for God sake…
We do not have time to waste with all the drama…

Treat someone bad and your get your karma…
When did dating become so bad…
Disappointed and guys making us sad…
Single and independent we should be glad…

Rape

Since when does someone think it is ok to take
advantage of a girl or guy…
Slipping date rape in to the drinks they buy…
Guys not taking no for an answer no matter how
hard we try…
Guys also affected and cry…
Rape…
Does not discriminate…
It can happen anywhere even on a date…
Why are women told we asked for it if we
dressed like that…
Those comments come from twats…
Girls should feel safe to walk home alone at
night…
And we should not be told to shout or you did
not put up a fight…
Or call for an officer in sight…
Guys also can be attacked…
This is also a fact…
Guys need to know it is ok to speak up if this
happens to you…
Report it and be brave is what you need to do…
I have lost count of the harassment I have had…
I have experienced lots of attacks which is truly
sad…
But I have carried on and for that I am glad…

I lose count of women feeling the same…
If something happened feeling they are to blame…
Women and men should feel safe in taxis and going home…
Feel safe to be alone…
And not have to take pictures of the licence plate on our phone…
Instead of telling girls we need to not be alone and put up more of a fight…
Drum it in to your children sexual assault is never right…
No matter what the situation ok…
What else do we need to say…
Talk to your children so they understand consent ok…

Escape

Sound of sobbing through the tears…
Lying awake at night reliving my worst fears…
Sometimes I sit and wonder…
Is this all life has to offer…
Watching the world go by and ponder…
He rises from his curse bed…
With thoughts of violence in his head…
A flash of rage and he sees red…
Without a pause I turned and fled…

Don't Give Up

If you ever find yourself one the edge of life…
Cannot cope with any more trouble, pain or strife…
Just know nothing is worth giving up hope…
Even if you feel you can no longer cope…
You can always back track…
You can get your life back…
Just do not cross that line of no return ok…
Hold on for one more day…
Just do not give up today…
Life has a way of turning around…
A new life will be found…
Sometimes we need to trust the process the universe is sending…
Even if it seems hopeless, I promise there is a happier ending…

Free

Do something crazy today...
Open the door and let the sunlight lead the way...
The feel of the wind through your hair...
Letting go of any despair...
Beautiful ocean blue sky...
Feeling free like a bird who can fly...
Trees dancing in the breeze…
Crisp golden leaves…
Happiness comes to those who believe...

Hey You

Hey you…
I see you I really do…
That amazing strong light…
Holding on through the fight…
Is such a beautiful sight…
You inspire me…
Make me want to do better and strive for where I want to be…
I look up to you…
In everything that you do…
My hero that is true…

Nature Hugs

If life gives you a million reasons to break down
and cry…
And you just want to break down and sigh…
Show the world you are strong and get back up
and try…
When you are on your knees…
And nobody sees…
Look at the beautiful flowers and bees…
Because if we have nothing else, we have the
beauty of the world around us…
Getting close to nature and walks is a must…
So go for a walk in the woods and listen to the
birds singing…
Listen to the sound of nature ringing…
Sit down and close your eyes…
Beauty of the world never lies…
If we feel like we have nobody and are all
alone…
Go to the beach and hear the waves crash and
moan…
If we look around and really see…
I am never alone as I have nature with me…

Who To Be

Be the vision…
Trust every decision…
Be the purpose and light…
Trust everything will work out alright…
Be your own best friend…
Trust that you can heal and mend…
Be your own superhero who is strong…
Trust nothing bad happens for too long…
Be honest and true…
Always be you…
Be bold and courageous...
Positivity is contagious…
Be brave…
Never cave…
Be everything you need…
Believe in yourself and you will succeed…
Always believe in oneself…
Be true and kind to yourself...

Believe

They told me it was not possible to do…
Show them I can do anything I put my mind
too…
Your thoughts are powerful and strong…
You will reach your goals it won't be too long…
Do not let anyone put you down or make you
feel low…
It is ok to say no…
Block out the noise and jealousy right now…
Never throw in the towel…
keep going as you are…
As that will get you far…
You attract the world with your smile...
You stand out by a mile...
You do not see how gorgeous you really are...
Infectious laugh echoing far…
Guitar playing just the way you are…

www.ingramcontent.com/pod-product-compliance
Lightning Source LLC
Chambersburg PA
CBHW051751130826
49812CB00033B/1092
* 9 7 8 9 3 5 7 6 9 9 2 5 9 *